EXPERIENCING JEWISH PRAYER

JOEL LURIE GRISHAVER

TORAH AURA PRODUCTIONS

ISBN: 978–1–934527–6722

Copyright © 2012 Torah Aura Productions. All rights reserved.

No part of this publication may be reproduced or transmitted in any form or by any means graphic, electronic or mechanical, including photocopying, recording or by any information storage and retrieval system, without permission in writing from the publisher.

Torah Aura Productions • 4423 Fruitland Avenue, Los Angeles, CA 90058
(800) BE-Torah • (800) 238-6724 • (323) 585-7312 • fax (323) 585-0327
E-MAIL <misrad@torahaura.com> • Visit the Torah Aura website at www.torahaura.com

Manufactured in China

Contents

God Thoughts

God. Even though this is a book about prayer, you can't think about prayer without dealing with God. To be able to pray, or to figure out what the siddur (prayerbook) means to us, we need to know what we think about God. If we are on one side of the dialogue, we need to know who we think is listening.

Here are some quick looks at some common ways people believe in God.

eXperience

CIRCLE THE IDEA THAT IS CLOSEST TO YOUR BELIEF. WRITE AND DRAW ONE IF NONE OF THESE IS CLOSE.

The Puppet

God pulls strings. God controls the world, setting people's futures and working miracles.

The Watchmaker

A watchmaker makes a watch. He puts it together, winds it up and then leaves it running. God works the same way. God created the world and then left it running.

Making a List and Checking It Twice

God takes notes on what we do. Later we'll get rewarded or punished for what we've done.

Jiminy Cricket— The Still, Small Voice

"Always let your conscience be your guide." God is like the small voice that whispers in our ears and hearts. God is the feeling that we are doing the right or wrong thing.

Share Any of Your Own.

Mother Nature, Scientific Laws, Natural Rules and Other Truth-of-Truths

God is a Higher Power made up of all the forces and principles that rule the world. God is order. God gives order.

PARTNER UP. SHARE YOUR BASIC GOD IDEA WITH YOUR PARTNER. THEN PARTNERS SHOULD REPORT YOUR GOD THOUGHTS TO THE WHOLE GROUP.

5

We can feel
God inside
us.

The God Game

There is
no God.

We can see
God in nature.

In the center of every page there is a question about God. In each corner there is an answer. Go to the corner of your room that matches the answer you like best. Talk with other people in your corner about why you chose that answer. There are five questions. You may be in a different group for each answer.

Question 1:

How do we know that there is a God?

We just have
to believe.

God dictated it to Moses on Mt. Sinai.

The God Game

God inspired people and they wrote down their understanding.

Wise people learned wisdom and wrote it down.

IN THE CENTER OF EVERY PAGE THERE IS A QUESTION ABOUT GOD. IN EACH CORNER THERE IS AN ANSWER. GO TO THE CORNER OF YOUR ROOM THAT MATCHES THE ANSWER YOU LIKE BEST. TALK WITH OTHER PEOPLE IN YOUR CORNER ABOUT WHY YOU CHOSE THAT ANSWER. THERE ARE FIVE QUESTIONS. YOU MAY BE IN A DIFFERENT GROUP FOR EACH ANSWER.

Question 2:

Does the Torah come from God?

Various people wrote stuff for various reasons and it got woven together.

Praying can make you feel better.

The God Game

Prayers can make God feel better, and that helps.

Praying is just boring.

IN THE CENTER OF EVERY PAGE THERE iS A QUESTION ABOUT GOD. IN EACH CORNER THERE iS AN ANSWER. GO TO THE CORNER OF YOUR ROOM THAT MATCHES THE ANSWER YOU LiKE BEST. TALK WiTH OTHER PEOPLE iN YOUR CORNER ABOUT WHY YOU CHOSE THAT ANSWER. THERE ARE FiVE QUESTIONS. YOU MAY BE iN A DiFFERENT GROUP FOR EACH ANSWER.

Question 3:

Does praying make a difference?

Prayers can make a sick person well.

What goes
around
comes around
(karma).

The
God
Game

Good people invite
other people to be
good and vice versa.

God rewards and punishes (eventually).

IN THE CENTER OF EVERY PAGE THERE IS A QUESTION ABOUT GOD. IN EACH CORNER THERE IS AN ANSWER. GO TO THE CORNER OF YOUR ROOM THAT MATCHES THE ANSWER YOU LIKE BEST. TALK WITH OTHER PEOPLE IN YOUR CORNER ABOUT WHY YOU CHOSE THAT ANSWER. THERE ARE FIVE QUESTIONS. YOU MAY BE IN A DIFFERENT GROUP FOR EACH ANSWER.

Question 4:

Do good people get rewarded and bad people punished?

Only by accident.

You live on
in people's
memories.

Reincarnation.

The
God
Game

A worm farm (nothing).

In the center of every page there is a question about God. In each corner there is an answer. Go to the corner of your room that matches the answer you like best. Talk with other people in your corner about why you chose that answer. There are five questions. You may be in a different group for each answer.

Question 5:

What happens after you die?

Some version of Heaven and Hell.

God and Prayer

Let's look at four different ways our belief in God can intersect with our belief in prayer.

If we believe in God, it is easy to pray. We can think of prayers as really talking to our Deity, really asking for things we might get, or we can think of praying as our talking to God to find out what we *should* want. After all, we can talk to God in the exact same way we can talk to a friend or parent in order to work out a problem.

We can pray as if there is a God (even if we're not sure). It is sometimes easier to tell things, admit things to someone else—that is the "why" behind imaginary friends. We can assume/pretend that there is a God because that makes praying easier. Kurt Vonnegut teaches, in a book called *Cat's Cradle*, "A perfectly useful religion can be built out of lies."

Even if we don't believe in God (or in a God who can listen and respond to prayer), here is still a way to use the liturgy. We can think of the service as a chance to be with the community, or as a chance to reflect. The prayers can be me asking myself for things, rather than having God involved.

We don't know if there really is a God or not. Either way it can't hurt us to pray; but if there is a God, and we don't, we might be in trouble. It is the same reason we walk around ladders. We don't really believe, but…

Or you just may not want to pray at all.

A Prayer Story:
The Horse Who Could Pray

One man shouted, "I'll bet you ten kopeck you can't."

The stranger shouted, "I'll bet you ten kopeck I can."

A third man shouted, "Five more kopeck says you can't."

Then the rabbi walked in and asked, "What is going on here?"

The first man said, "This man says he can teach my horse to pray. He says that he can make him pray just like any other Jew. I bet him he can't."

Seven different men said, "So did I."

The rabbi said, "A praying horse is something I would like to see. It might teach all of you something."

The stranger took the horse. He went away for a month. Then the day came. He and the horse were standing in the back of the synagogue. Everyone else was standing, too. There was no room to sit. Everyone in the whole town was there. Everyone from miles away was there, too. Everyone wanted to see the horse that could pray.

The stranger picked up a huge siddur. He held it up for everyone to see. He said, "I have taught this horse the seder of the service." The stranger took the siddur and placed it on the *shtandard*. A *shtandard* is the desk that some Jews use as a table to hold books when they pray or study. He put a kippah and a tallit on the horse.

Someone joked, "Now the horse looks like a Jew. But can he pray like a Jew?"

The horse went over to the shtandard. He looked in the siddur. He bowed his head up and down, up and down. After a little while he put his nose into the siddur and turned the page. Then he did it again and again. The horse's head went up and down, up and down. Then the horse turned the page. He looked just like a Jew who was really praying.

The man said, "I have won the bet."

The rabbi walked over and patted the horse. Then he

walked over to the *shtandard*. He picked up the siddur and shook it. Oats, lots of oats, fell out of the pages. Everyone in the synagogue laughed.

The rabbi said, "Don't laugh so hard. The horse prays the way most of you do. The horse knows how to turn the pages. The horse knows how to follow the order. But the horse does not know how to have his heart in his prayers. Still, the horse does pray better than some of you."

 DID THE STRANGER WIN OR LOSE THE BET? WHAT DOES IT TAKE TO REALLY HAVE YOUR HEART IN A PRAYER?

 ACT OUT THIS STORY.

Hevruta Texts on Prayer

WORK WITH A HEVRUTA PARTNER AND READ THESE TEXTS. PUT AN "X" THROUGH THOSE TEXTS WITH WHICH YOU DISAGREE. PICK YOUR FAVORITE TEXT.

[1] Prayer...gives us the opportunity to be honest, to say what we believe, and to stand for what we say. —Abraham Joshua Heschel

[2] Every wish is like a prayer to God. —Elizabeth Barrett Browning

[3] Prayer...teaches people to overcome bitterness and self-pity, to think not of what the world owes him/her, but what he or she owes the world and God. —Solomon B. Freehof

[4] Prayer cannot mend a broken bridge, rebuild a ruined city, or bring water to parched fields. Prayer can mend a broken heart, lift up a discouraged soul, and strengthen a weakened will. —Ferdinand M. Isserman

[5] To pray is to feel and give expression to a deep sense of gratitude. No intelligent, healthy, normal human being should take for granted...the innumerable blessings which God... bestows upon him or her daily, the blessings of parents, loved ones, of friends and country, of health and understanding. —Simon Greenberg

[6] When I was young, I asked my father, "If you don't believe in God, why do you go to synagogue so regularly?" My father answered, "Jews go to synagogue for all kinds of reasons. My friend Garfinkle, who is Orthodox, goes to talk to God. I go to talk to Garfinkle." —Harry Golden

[7] Prayer in Judaism… is bound up with human needs, wants, drives, and urges…Prayer tells the individual as well as the community, what his/her or its genuine needs are, what s/he should, or should not, petition God about… —Rabbi Joseph Soleveitchik

[8] If prayer worked the way most people think it does, no one would ever die, because no prayer is offered more sincerely than a prayer for life, for health and recovery from illness, for ourselves and for those we love… People who pray for miracles usually don't get miracles any more than children who pray for bicycles, good grades, or boyfriends get them as a result of praying. But people who pray for courage, for strength to bear the unbearable, for grace to remember what they have left instead of what they have lost, very often find their prayers answered. They discover that they have more strength, more courage than they ever knew themselves to have. —Rabbi Harold Kushner

the contract to study prayer

I, _____ [the teacher], promise to use all my knowledge, skills and talents to make this course interesting.

I promise not to try to convince you that you should pray or to try to make you feel guilty if you don't go to services regularly. (But if you happen to pray, I won't make you feel bad either.) however, I also promise to try to interest you in the siddur (prayerbook) and to show you ways it can be useful.

finally, I promise to give you lots of opportunities to talk about your feelings and beliefs about prayer, god, and other important issues.

I, _____ [the student], promise to willingly suspend my disbelief (and listen with an open mind to lessons) about prayer, god, and other such questions, long enough for my teacher to present some new information about the siddur and the words that it contains.

I also promise to do my best to understand how jewish services work, and to try to figure out the lessons that they teach. I will do so in order to gain all of the background possible in order to make my own descision about the important prayers in my own life.

finally, I also promise to be open about my feelings and beliefs. I will explore them, admit the questions and doubts I have, and allow my understandings to grow.

[the teacher] _____

[the student] _____

I think it was a ten- or eleven-year-old Ari who said, "I get it. The service is sort of like a car wash. First one thing comes down and spins around. Then another thing does its job spraying something. The parts all work in order, and each one does something. When it is done, the car that comes out is different from the way it went in."

Jewish Worship Is Not a Spectator Sport– It Is an Audience Participation Game

 MAKE A TEAM OF STUDENTS AND USE YOUR BODIES TO CREATE A MOVING SCULPTURE OF A WORKING CAR WASH.

The Anatomy of a Brakhah

Long Brakhah

Petiḥta

בָּרוּךְ אַתָּה יי אֱלֹהֵינוּ מֶלֶךְ הָעוֹלָם...

Barukh Attah Adonai Eloheinu Melekh ha-Olam...

Body

XXXXX XX XXXXXXX XXXX XXXX XXX XXXXX XX
XXXXXXX XXXX XXXX XXX XXXXX XX XXXXXXX XXXX
XXXX XXX XXXXX XX XXXXXXX XXXX XXXX XXX XXXXX
XX XXXXXXX XXXX XXXX XXX XXXXX XX XXXXXX
XXXX XXXX XXX

Ḥatimah

בָּרוּךְ אַתָּה יי... ...*Barukh Attah Adonai...*
XXXXX XX XXXX XXXXXX XXXXX.

Short Brakhah

Body

XXXXX XX XXXXXXX XXXX XXXX XXX XXXXX XX
XXXXXXX XXXX XXXX XXX XXXXX XX XXXXXXX XXXX
XXXX XXX XXXXX XX XXXXXXX XXXX XXXX XXX XXXXX
XX XXXXXXX XXXX XXXX XXX XXXXX XX XXXXXXX
XXXX XXXX XXX

Ḥatimah

בָּרוּךְ אַתָּה יי... ...*Barukh Attah Adonai...*
XXXXX XX XXXX XXXXXX XXXXX.

PETIḤTA comes from the Hebrew word פּוֹתֵחַ *pota'aḥ*, which means "open." It is the technical name for the opening *brakhah*-formula. It must have all three parts: *Barukh* (בָּרוּךְ) *Shem* (אַתָּה יי) and *Malkhut* (אֱלֹהֵינוּ מֶלֶךְ הָעוֹלָם).

ḤATIMAH comes from the Hebrew word חוֹתֵם *ḥotem*, which means "seal" (as in pour hot wax on a document, then stamping it with the seal to make it official). The Ḥatimah is closing brakhah-formula (that is minus *Malkhut*) that ends every brakhah, both long and short.

23

Brakhot Are Organized Like a Train

GET COPIES OF THE SIDDUR YOUR CONGREGATION USES. WORK WITH A PARTNER. FIND THE SHEMA IN AN EVENING SERVICE. CHECK OUT THE BRAKHOT BEFORE AND AFTER IT. ARE THEY LONG OR SHORT? THEN DO THE SAME FOR THE MORNING SERVICE.

Evening		Long	Short
מַעֲרִיב עֲרָבִים	Ma'ariv Aravim		
אַהֲבַת עוֹלָם	Ahavat Olam		
שְׁמַע	Shema		
גְּאֻלָּה	G'ulah		
הַשְׁכִּיבֵנוּ	Haskiveynu		

Morning		Long	Short
יוֹצֵר אוֹר	Yotzer Or		
אַהֲבָה רַבָּה	Ahavah Rabbah		
שְׁמַע	Shema		
גְּאֻלָּה	G'ulah		

A long blessing includes the words אֱלֹהֵינוּ מֶלֶךְ הָעוֹלָם *Eloheinu Melekh ha-Olam*. A short blessing does not. A short blessing is also called "a blessing resting on its neighbor," because every blessing needs a connection to **Malkhut** (*Eloheinu Melekh ha-Olam*), and a short blessing gets it by making the closing-*barukh* of the previous blessing into its opening blessing. This makes a chain of *brakhot* like a train. The long *brakhah* at the beginning is the engine pulling the rest of the cars.

CREATE A TEAM. GRAB A SIDDUR AND USE YOUR BODIES TO TURN THE EVENING SHEMA AND ITS BLESSING INTO A TRAIN.

The Five Parts of Services

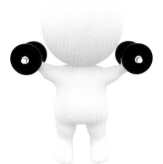

1. The Warmup

The warmup is the stretching and toning part of the service. It is the part that changes the most between different services. While each service has a different structure for the warmup, the warmup sets the mood and helps us get ourselves ready for the worship workout.

Creation
Revelation
שְׁמַע
Redemption

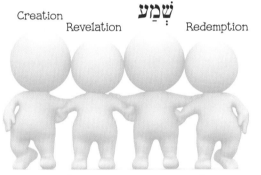

2. The Shema-&-Her-Brakhot

This is a cycle of three (morning) and four (evening) *brakhot* that surround three passages from the Torah—the Shema. These brakhot surround the Shema and deal with the three big themes in the Jewish Experience: the **creation** of the world, the **revelation** of the Torah, and the **redemption** of the Jewish people from Egypt (and in the future). They surround the most central Jewish idea—that there is One God.

3. The Amidah

The *Amidah* is a chain of nineteen *brakhot* (eighteen or less in most Reform siddurim), seven *brakhot* on Shabbat and eight on holidays. Even though the number of *brakhot* in the *Amidah* changes, it is always an *Amidah* sandwich with the same three opening *brakhot*, the same three closing *brakhot*, and one to thirteen *brakhot* as the filling in the middle. During the week these middle *brakhot* are a shopping list, voicing our deepest needs to God.

KOOM-BA-YAH!

4. The Torah Service

The Torah service is the public learning experience. Throughout the rest of the service we spend our time talking to God. The Torah service is when God talks to us—this is where God's message is read.

5. The Concluding Service

The concluding service, the finale, wraps up the service. It always includes the *Aleinu* (that is the service's reprise of all the great themes in the service) and some communal good and welfare—the mourner's kaddish. Closing songs and benedictions and extra prayers are part of the shut-down procedure for some services.

eXperience WORK WITH YOUR TEAM AND CREATE A MOVING MACHINE THAT CONNECTS THESE FIVE PARTS INTO A COMPLETE SERVICE.

eXperience | LIST AS MANY THINGS AS YOU CAN THAT ONE SHOULD THINK ABOUT BEFORE GOING INTO WORSHIP SERVICES.

Think about going to a baseball practice

(Swimming, aerobics, tennis, basketball, gymnastics, lacrosse, luge, football or ballet will work as well.)

Before you start working out, you **warmup**. You stretch. You do some jumping jacks. You get your body ready for the demands of the practice and the game.

Services begin the same way. Before we get to the real spiritual workout, we do some **warmup** prayers.

Four Services—Four Warmups

NOTE: There are many different Orthodox prayerbooks; most make changes by adding things. The Conservative and Reconstructionist movements tend to change words but leave the structure of the prayers intact. The Reform movement (Progressive Judaism) and Renewal congregations are different. Sometimes they follow the traditional structure; sometimes they are creative. Match the following material to your congregational siddur.

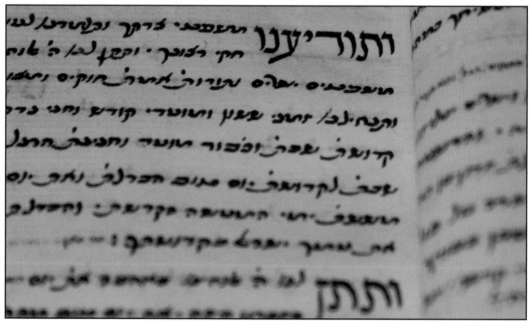

Ma'ariv—The Evening Service

Evening services start with a cry for help. In just two sentences (Psalms 70:38, Psalms 20:10) we say: "Have mercy! Please don't get mad at us! Please listen." It isn't so much a warmup as it is an explosion out of the starting block. It is called by its first words *V'Hu Ra<u>h</u>um*.

Rabbi Stuart Kelman teaches: "Evening services were short because night was a scary time and people wanted to get home as soon after dark as they could."

ACT OUT A IN A PANTOMIME A PERSON WALKING HOME THROUGH THE THINGS THAT GO BUMP IN THE NIGHT. SHOW HOW COMING HOME IN THE DARK CAN BE SCARY.

Sha<u>h</u>arit—Morning Service

The morning service has the longest warmup section. It actually has two warmup parts. First come *Birkhot ha-Sha<u>h</u>ar* (the morning blessings); then comes *P'sukei d'Zimra* (sentences of song).

Birkhot ha-Sha<u>h</u>ar

Birkhot ha-Sha<u>h</u>ar is like the exercise equipment people have at home. It is supposed to be done regularly and often gets neglected. The Rabbis moved the service to synagogue (that is sort of like joining a gym).

In the middle of a lot of other material we find a list of morning blessings that were designed to accompany a wake-up ritual.

29

The Talmudic Wake-Up Ritual

Action	Blessing
Hearing Rooster	*Barukh Atah Adonai…* Who has given the rooster the intelligence to tell the difference between night and day.
Opening One's Eyes	*Barukh Atah Adonai…* Who opens the eyes of the blind.
Sitting Up	*Barukh Atah Adonai…* Who frees the captive.
Getting Dressed	*Barukh Atah Adonai…* Who clothes the naked.
Getting Out of Bed	*Barukh Atah Adonai…* Who lifts up the fallen.
Putting Feet on Ground	*Barukh Atah Adonai…* Who spreads the land over the water.
Beginning to Walk	*Barukh Atah Adonai…* Who makes firm each person's steps.
Tying One's Shoes	*Barukh Atah Adonai…* Who meets all my needs.
Closing the Belt	*Barukh Atah Adonai…* Who girds Israel with strength.
Who Covers His/Her Head	*Barukh Atah Adonai…* Who crowns Israel with glory.

Brakhot 60a

 IN SMALL GROUPS FIGURE OUT THE CONNECTION BETWEEN THE ACTIONS AND THE BLESSINGS. THEN GO BACK AND WRITE BLESSINGS TO GO WITH YOUR WAKE-UP RITUAL. SHARE.

 WRITE A LiST OF THE STEPS iNVOLVED iN GOiNG FROM WAKING UP TO BEiNG READY FOR THE DAY.

Step	Blessing
1. Be awakened by _____	_____ _____
2. _____	_____ _____
3. _____	_____ _____
4. _____	_____ _____
5. _____	_____ _____
6. _____	_____ _____
7. _____	_____ _____
8. _____	_____ _____
9. _____	_____ _____
10. _____	_____ _____

The Rabbinic Wake-Up Ritual

Experience

I tie my shoes

Say Brakhah

"Who meets all
my needs."

What God Does

God helps people

What I Can Do

I must help people.

A stimulus is something that happens to you. A response is what you do about it. Some responses are automatic, and some are trained. You can train a response through repetition.

The Schulweis Lesson

Rabbi Harold Schulweis teaches that a Jew should add the words "through me" to every brakhah. Because we are created in God's image, we should take each of the things we praise God for doing and set them as our own goals. That is real praise.

> Praised are You...Who frees the captives.

becomes

> Praised are You...Who frees the captives through me.

The Computer Blessing

Write a blessing and a Schulweis blessing for booting your computer.

_____

_____

_____

Birkhot ha-Sha<u>h</u>ar
The Brakhot of Dawn

This service was originally a home ritual. Slowly it evolved into a synagogue process. It includes:

Mah Tovu, a welcome to synagogue prayer.

Adon Olam/Yigdal, God-is-great songs

A Hand-Washing Brakhah

An After-the-Bathroom Brakhah

Two Torah Brakhot

A Talmud Text to Study (Shabbat 127a)

Elohai N'shamah (A thank-you-for-letting-me-wake-up brakhah)

Birkhot ha-Sha<u>h</u>ar, the string of waking-up-and-getting-dressed brakhot

Study Texts, an assortment of texts, including the Binding of Isaac, the Shema, Rules of Sacrifice.

The Rabbis' Kaddish, which defines the end of the study session.

Psalm 30, a preparation for P'sukei d'Zimra.

The Mourner's Kaddish, the gathering of a minyan and a transition.

Along the way we also do brakhot over **tallit** and **tefillin**.

P'Sukei D'Zimra
Sentences of Song

P'sukei d'Zimra is essentially a "God is Great" songfest. Originally P'sukei d'Zimra was only the last six Psalms (145–150). Today it has grown to include:

Barukh she-Amar, An opening brakhah.

Hodu L'Adonai, a Praise passage from 1 Chronicles 16:8-36.

Mizmor l'Todah, Psalm 100.

Yehi Kavod, a compilation of Psalm verses.

Ashrei, Psalms 145 plus two other verses.

Psalms 146–150

Va y'Varaekh David, 1 Chronicles 29:10–13.

Atah Hu Adonai, Nehemiah 9.6–11.

Shirat ha-Yam, The Song of the Sea, Exodus 14:30–15.19.

Yishtaba<u>h</u>, a closing brakhah.

<u>H</u>atzi Kaddish, an ending and transition.

 INSTANT PSALM: GIVE A 3"×5" CARD TO EVERYONE IN THE CLASS. ON IT EACH PERSON SHOULD WRITE ONE SENTENCE THAT "TELLS OF THE GREAT THINGS THAT GOD HAS DONE." GATHER IN GROUPS. POOL YOUR CARDS AND ARRANGE THEM IN THE RIGHT ORDER TO BE A PSALM.

Mussaf—The Extra Service

On Shabbat and Holidays there is an extra service. (*Mussaf*). *Mussaf* follows the morning service and its Torah service. By that point people are already warmed up. That is why there is no specific warmup for *Mussaf*.

Minhah

Minhah is the afternoon service. In the Temple it was a separate service. Today, in most synagogues, it is run just before *Ma'ariv*.

The *Ashrei* is the warmup to *Minhah*. The *Ashrei* is made of Psalms 145 and an introduction taken from other Psalms (84.5, 114.15). It is an acrostic—that is, an alef-to-tav (a–z) prayer. Its only surprise is that the נ *nun* is missing.

The *Ashrei* is said three times a day. It is said during morning services as part of the *P'sukei d'Zimra*, the verses of song, and again after the *Tefillah* (*Amidah*). It is said for a third time at the beginning of the *Minhah* (afternoon) service. When we say the *Ashrei* as part of the Torah service on Shabbat we are actually beginning the *Mussaf* service (and replacing the weekday *Ashrei* that came after the *Tefillah*). We do not say *Ashrei* at evening services.

A-Z Praise

eXperience WORK WITH A PARTNER TO WRITE AN A-Z PRAISE OF GOD.

a. _____

b. _____

c. _____

d. _____

e. _____

f. _____

g. _____

h. _____

i. _____

j. _____

k. _____

l. _____

m. _____

o. _____

p. _____

q. _____

r. _____

s. _____

t. _____

u. _____

v. _____

w. _____

x. _____

y. _____

z. _____

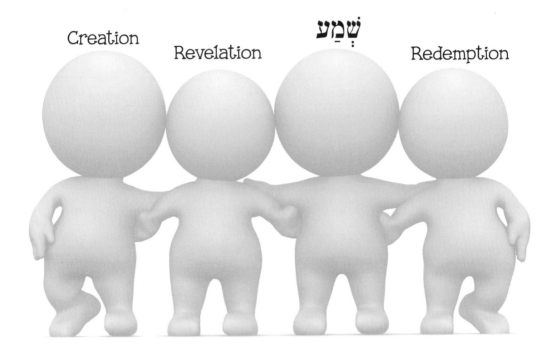

Creation

Revelation

שְׁמַע

Redemption

בָּרְכוּ **Barekhu:** The *Barekhu* is a stand-alone part of the service. It is not part of the warmup and not part of the "Shema-&-Her-Blessings." It is a very short section called the *Zimun*, the invitation. It is here that the congregation becomes a community—because the *Barekhu* requires a minyan.

The *Barekhu* is call-and-response. The leader says the first line and bows, then the community responds with the second line and then bows.

CALL-AND-RESPONSE

WORK WITH A GROUP TO WRITE YOUR OWN SERVICE BEGINNING THAT IS A CALL-AND-RESPONSE. MAKE IT SOMETHING THAT THE LEADER SAYS AND TO WHICH THE CONGREGATION RESPONDS. MAKE IT SOMETHING THAT GATHERS EVERYONE TOGETHER AND STARTS THE SERVICE. PEFORM YOUR OPENING FOR YOUR CLASS.

Shema

The Birth of the Shema

Once, when the Temple in Jerusalem was still the central place for Jewish worship, there was no *Shema*. The parts were indeed already in the Torah, but they had not yet been brought together and turned into a prayer. In those days the Ten Commandments were a central part of the worship service.

Eventually the daily use of the Ten Commandments as the central part of the service began to cause some major problems. Jews began to think that some commandments (the ten) were more important than the rest of the 613 mitzvot in the Torah. They said, "The Ten Commandments are more important than the rest, and we can be good Jews by only doing (and not doing) those."

To keep people from thinking that the Ten Commandments were the only important commandments, the officials who ran the Temple service dropped the Ten Commandments from the daily service and replaced them with a collection of passages named after the first word in the first passage: *Shema*.

Back when the Temple was still the place to worship and sacrifices were the best way to get in touch with God, the *Shema* was already important. In fact, it was the most important thing in the Jewish prayer service.

 THE SHEMA IS CALLED "THE WATCHWORD OF OUR FAITH." WHAT DOES THAT MEAN?

Oneness

eXperience WORK WITH A GROUP AND BRAINSTORM A LIST OF AS MANY THINGS AS YOU CAN THAT ARE LIKE GOD IN THAT THEY ARE EVERYWHERE (OR LOTS OF WHERES) AND ARE STILL ONE.

_____

_____

_____

_____

_____

_____

_____

_____

_____

_____

_____

_____

_____

_____

_____

_____

_____

The Pattern

 TAKE A SIDDUR. PUT A BOOKMARK AT THE *BAREKHU* FOR THE EVENING SERVICE AND ANOTHER FOR THE MORNING *BAREKHU*.

Prayer	Evening Theme	Morning Theme	Long or Short	Page #
The First Prayer after the *Barekhu*				
The Second Prayer after the *Barekhu*				
Shema				
The First Prayer after the Shema				
The Second Prayer after the Shema				

Define these words through matching:

Creation   God saves the world and rescues all people.

Revelation   God makes everything that exists.

Redemption   God teaches people about our purpose (Torah).

Put these themes in the right order:

☐ Redemption   ☐ Creation   ☐ Revelation

 USE YOUR BODIES TO MAKE THE SHEMA-&-HER-BLESSINGS CARWASH AGAIN.

Creation

 FORM A GROUP. IMAGINE THAT YOUR GROUP CAN MAKE DECISIONS FOR GOD. WHAT WOULD YOU CREATE ON EACH OF THE SEVEN DAYS OF CREATION?

Day One	
Day Two	
Day Three	
Day Four	
Day Five	
Day Six	
The Seventh Day	

Creation Blessings

מַעֲרִיב עֲרָבִים *Ma'ariv Aravim* is the first blessing before the Shema in the evening. It is the creation *brakhah*. It teaches us that time doesn't just happen, One day doesn't automatically follow the next. It teaches us that God has to remake and recreate everything every day. The *Ma'ariv* says "thanks for today" and "thanks for tomorrow." Not only do we thank God for everything created. It also forces us to ask, "Am I using my time well?"

 **WHAT IS THE CONNECTION BETWEEN CREATION AND TIME?**

יוֹצֵר אוֹר *Yotzer Or* is the first blessing before the Shema in the morning. It, too, is the creation *brakhah*. *Yotzer Or* is a sunrise blessing. In the traditional *siddur* (in the Conservative siddur, too) it is a blessing that takes a number of pages with a lot of parts. (In the Reform siddur it is shortened to one paragraph.) *Yotzer Or* deals with day and night, light and dark, and good and evil. The world is made up of all these pairs. Darkness isn't an evil; it just doesn't have light. Likewise, evil is simply where the force of God hasn't yet reached.

reflection question **WHERE DOES EVIL COME FROM?**

Creation Prayer

eXperience | WRITE A SENTENCE FOR A PRAYER ON CREATION.

_____

_____

eXperience | TAKE SIX MORE SENTENCES FROM THE REST OF YOUR CLASS AND CREATE A PRAYER OF CREATION.

_____

_____

_____

_____

_____

_____

_____

_____

_____

_____

_____

_____

Revelation

List of Truths

eXperience WORK WITH A GROUP AND BRAINSTORM A LIST OF AS MANY THINGS AS YOU CAN THINK OF THAT ARE COMPLETELY TRUE.

_____

_____

_____

_____

_____

_____

_____

_____

_____

_____

_____

_____

_____

_____

_____

_____

_____

Revelation Blessings

אַהֲבַת עוֹלָם *Ahavat Olam* is the second blessing before the Shema in the evening service. Its theme is revelation, and it is like a visit to Mount Sinai. It makes the connection between the rules of the Torah (the positives and the negatives) and God's love for us. Among other metaphors, Torah is a gift to us from God, and it is the wedding contract between us and God. The words of *Ahavat Olam* are drawn from Jeremiah's Book of Comfort.

 **WHAT CONNECTS TORAH AND LOVE?**

אַהֲבָה רַבָּה *Ahavah Rabbah* is the morning version of *Ahavat Olam*. It, too, is a prayer about revelation that connects love and law. Saadia Gaon points out that while the creation *brakhot* talk about God in the third person, these revelation *brakhot* talk about God in the second person. We have gotten closer. Torah is the *ketubah*, the wedding contract, between Israel and God.

 **HOW IS IT DIFFERENT TO TALK ABOUT GOD IN THE SECOND PERSON RATHER THAN IN THE THIRD PERSON?**

Top Commandments

THE TORAH BRAKHOT ARE ALL ABOUT MITZVOT, COMMANDMENTS. WRITE DOWN A MITZVAH FROM THE TORAH THAT YOU THINK IS ONE OF THE MOST IMPORTANT IN THE TORAH. THEN WORK AS A CLASS TO VOTE FOR YOUR TOP TEN MITZVOT.

_____

_____

_____

Redemption Brakhot

The Evening גְּאֻלָּה G'ulah

The *G'ulah* is the first blessing after the *Shema*. It is the redemption *brakhah*. The *G'ulah* is set at the Reed Sea. The *G'ulah* uses the historical memory of the exodus from Egypt as the promise that a bigger redemption will come in the future. The prayer uses a number of passages from Exodus, from the moment of crossing the Reed Sea. It ends with a passage from Jeremiah: "The Eternal will free Jacob and redeem him from a hand mightier than his own."

 HOW DOES ONE REDEMPTION PROMISE THE NEXT?

הַשְׁכִּיבֵנוּ *Hashkiveinu*

Hashkiveinu is a blessing that should not exist. It breaks the symmetry of two blessings before the *Shema* and one blessing after it. It is an extra blessing that extends the evening *G'ulah* to cover "the things that go bump in the night." It is a prayer about fear of the dark. We ask to be protected all night.

 HOW IS PRAYING AT NIGHT DIFFERENT THAN PRAYING DURING THE DAY?

The Morning גְּאֻלָּה G'ulah

The morning redemption *brakhah* the first after the *Shema*, is also called the *G'ulah*. It, too, is a recreation of the singing that Israel did on the banks of the Reed Sea. In the Bible (Exodus 15:1–18), Moses and Israel and Miriam and the Women of Israel sing a song. When we sing the *G'ulah* we sing back and forth between the congregation and the prayer leader. This is an acting out of the Song of the Sea. Again, the celebration of this first redemption is taken as the promise of a future redemption.

WHY DOES THE TRADITION SET UP PRAYERS THAT WE ACT OUT?

The Song of Redemption

The *G'ulah* is connected to the redemption from Egypt. It is best defined by the Song of the Sea that Moses sang with the men while Miriam led the women in song.

BRAINSTORM IN A SMALL GROUP TEN THINGS THAT WILL HAPPEN DURING THE FINAL REDEMPTION. MAKE THEM YOUR IDEA OF A PERFECT WORLD.

1. _____ 2. _____

3. _____ 4. _____

5. _____ 6. _____

7. _____ 8. _____

9. _____ 10. _____

NOW WRITE YOUR OWN SONG OF REDEMPTION. MAKE IT AN ECHO SONG THAT ONE PERSON LEADS AND EVERYONE ELSE REPEATS.

Bump in the Night

Hashkiveinu is a prayer that asks God to "help us make it through the night."

eXperience | WITH A PARTNER, MAKE A LIST OF AS MANY THINGS AS YOU CAN THINK OF THAT PEOPLE ARE SCARED OF AFTER DARK.

_____

_____

_____

_____

_____

_____

_____

_____

_____

_____

_____

_____

_____

_____

_____

_____

_____

The Amidah

The Structure of the עֲמִידָה Amidah

The *Amidah* is a silent prayer that is said standing, however, not all synagogues do it silently and it is not always all said standing. During the week it is usually made up of nineteen blessings. On Shabbat this is cut back to seven blessings.

The first three blessings are always the same. So are the last three (more or less). During the week there are thirteen middle blessings. On Shabbat there is only one.

PRAISE

The first three *brakhot* in the *Amidah* are about praise. Before we ask God for things we need, we tell God how wonderful God is.

1. אָבוֹת **Avot** You are the One Who Did Good for our ancestors.

2. גְּבוּרוֹת **G'vurot** You are our Hero.

3. קְדוּשָׁה **K'dushah** You are the source of our holiness.

DO AN IMAGINARY "SHOW AND TELL" ABOUT GOD. EVERYONE SHOULD BRING IN THREE IMAGINARY OBJECTS THAT SHOW GOD IS GREAT.

RABBI HANINAH SAID, THE FIRST THREE *BRAKHOT* OF THE *AMIDAH* ARE LIKE A SLAVE PRAISING HIS OR HER MASTER. WHAT METAPHOR WOULD YOU USE TO DESCRIBE THESE *BRAKHOT*?

PETITION

The middle thirteen brakhot in the *Amidah* are prayers that ask God to do things for us. They are a series of requests for things we need.

4. בִּינָה *Binah* We need wisdom.

5. תְּשׁוּבָה *T'shuvah* We need repentence.

6. סְלִיחָה *Slihah* We need Forgiveness.

7. גְּאֻלָּה *G'ulah* We need redemption.

8. רְפוּאָה *Refu'ah* We need healing.

9. בִּרְכַּת הַשָּׁנִים *Birkat ha-Shanim* We need a year of blessings.

10. קִבּוּץ גָּלֻיּוֹת *Kibbutz Galuyyot* We need a return from exile.

11. דִּין *Din* We need justice.

12. בִּרְכַּת הַמִּינִים *Birkat ha-Minim* We need our enemies defeated (some synagogues skip this).

13. צַדִּיקִים *Tzadikim* We need righteous role models.

14. בִּנְיַן יְרוּשָׁלַיִם *Binyan Yerushaliyim* We need Jerusalem rebuilt.

15. מַלְכוּת בֵּית דָּוִד *Malkhut Bet David* We need the empire of David again.

16. שׁוֹמֵעַ תְּפִלָּה *Shomei'a Tefillah* We need our prayers heard.

 RABBI HANINAH SAID, THE NEXT THIRTEEN *BRAKHOT* OF THE *AMIDAH* ARE LIKE A SLAVE ASKING HIS OR HER MASTER FOR GIFTS. WHAT METAPHOR WOULD YOU USE TO DESCRIBE THESE *BRAKHOT*?

 LOOK AT THE LIST OF REQUESTS IN THE *AMIDAH*. PICK THE ONE THAT IS MOST IMPORTANT TO YOU. EXPLAIN TO A PARTNER WHY YOU CHOSE IT.

THANKSGIVING

The last three *brakhot* are labeled "thanksgiving." They say "thank you." The idea is that after asking for something, we say "thank you" immediately (and before anything happens). This can be a way of "buttering up" God, or it can be an act of faith. The last *brakhah*, *Birkat Shalom*, is really another request.

17. עֲבוֹדָה *Avodah* Thanks for letting us serve God.

18. הוֹדָאָה *Hoda'ah* Thanks for letting us praise God.

19. בִּרְכַּת שָׁלוֹם *Birkat Shalom* We need peace (Great Peace-Giver).

 HOW WOULD YOU EXPLAIN THE "THANKSGIVING" PART OF THE *AMIDAH*?

 WHAT IS YOUR THOUGHT ABOUT WHY "PEACE" IS THE LAST BLESSING IN THE *AMIDAH*?

 WORK IN SMALL GROUPS. TELL THE STORY OF HOW WORLD PEACE FINALLY COMES.

THE SHABBAT VARIATION

On Shabbat and the Festivals the middle thirteen, the petition *brakhot*, are not said. It doesn't seem right to demand or request God to act on a day of rest. So instead of saying those *brakhot* we say a single blessing that thanks God for the unqiue holiness of the Sabbath. On festivals we add two blessings.

 WHAT IS THE BEST THING ABOUT SHABBAT?

The *Amidah* Game

ON THESE PAGES YOU WILL FIND 19 SQUARES, ONE FOR EACH OF THE *BRAKHOT* IN THE *AMIDAH*. MAKE UP A LOGO (GRAPHIC IMAGE) FOR EACH BLESSING. THEN USE THESE IMAGES TO INVENT AN AMIDAH GAME.

1. אָבוֹת *Avot*

2. גְּבוּרוֹת *G'vurot*

3. קְדוּשָׁה *K'dushah*

4. בִּינָה *Binah*

5. תְּשׁוּבָה *T'shuvah*

6. סְלִיחָה *Sliḥah*

7. גְּאֻלָּה *G'ulah*

52

8. רְפוּאָה *Refu'ah*

9. בִּרְכַּת הַשָּׁנִים
Birkat ha-Shanim

10. קִבּוּץ גָּלֻיּוֹת
Kibbutz Galuyyot

11. דִּין *Din*

12. בִּרְכַּת הַמִּינִים
Birkat ha-Minim

13. צַדִּיקִים *Tzadikim*

1. בִּנְיַן יְרוּשָׁלַיִם
Binyan Yerushaliyim

15. מַלְכוּת בֵּית דָּוִד
Malkhut Bet David

1. שׁוֹמֵעַ תְּפִלָּה
Shomei'a Tefillah

17. עֲבוֹדָה *Avodah*

18. הוֹדָאָה *Hoda'ah*

19. בִּרְכַּת שָׁלוֹם
Birkat Shalom

1. Remember the Sabbath to make it holy. (Exodus 20:8)

2. And God blessed the seventh day and made it holy because on it God rested from all the work that God created by doing. (Genesis 2:3)

3. Know that the essence of the stars and planets and the completeness of tzedakah only happens on Shabbat. Thus it is written: "A sunny Shabbat day is tzedakah for the poor." (Talmud, Ta'anit 8b)

4. This means that tzedakah only has complete light through the light of Shabbat, and through the Shabbat light it shines like the sun. (Rebbe Nachman of Bratslav)

5. Shabbat said before the Holy One: Every day was given a partner (Sunday had Monday, Tuesday had Wednesday, and Thursday had Friday), but You did not give me one. The Holy One answered: Your partner is the community of Israel. (*Exodus Rabbah* 20:8)

6. Three things give insight into the (pleasures of the) world to come: Shabbat, the sun, and bodily functions. The Holy One said to Israel: A good gift have I for Israel and Shabbat is her name. Go and tell them. (Talmud, *Shabbat* 10b)

7. There was a ruler who prepared a special wedding canopy. It was intricately carved and adorned; the only thing missing was the bride. So, too, the world was created intricately and majestically, but the only thing missing was Shabbat. (Midrash *Genesis Rabbah* Chapter 10)

8. Shabbat is called shalom. (Zohar)

9. Resh Lakish said that on Shabbat eve everyone is given an extra soul, and when Shabbat leaves it is taken from him/her. (Talmud, *Beitza* 16a)

10. Sabbath has a flavor of Paradise about it. (Talmud, *Brakhot*)

11. One who observes Shabbat is like one who created it. (Mekhilta)

eXperience NOW WRITE A PRAYER FOR THE SABBATH DAY.

The History of the *Amidah*

Back when Israel was first its own country and kings like David and Solomon ran the show, there was only one Jewish Temple, the Temple in Jerusalem (shuls, synagogues and neighborhood temples came later). Jerusalem was the one and only place where Jews could go to worship. While they could come every day (just as we can), the big crowds came three times a year: Sukkot, Passover and Shavuot.

In the Temple the major form of worship was sacrifice. A sacrifice was a lot like a barbeque. A family would bring a sheep or cow or some other animal, bird, or even flour, and the *Kohanim* (priests) who ran the Temple would cook it on an open grill (that was called the altar.) With most sacrifices, after the food was cooked, the *Kohanim* and the family would eat most of it together, burning a little bit of it up as "God's portion." While all this was going on, people would say their prayers, thanking God for the blessings that they had experience in their lives and asking God for the things they felt they needed.

When sacrifices happened all day, every day, the worship experience in the Temple was built around three major services. A sunrise service was called *Shaharit* (meaning "dawn"), an afternoon service was called *Minhah* ("rest hour") and an evening service was called *Ma'ariv* (meaning "evening.") On Shabbat and Festivals an extra service called *Mussaf* (meaning "added") was also celebrated.

Sometime before 586 B.C.E. Jews felt that they needed a local worship experience, too. Going to Jerusalem three times a year just wasn't enough. Some kind of local worship place (a kind of synagogue) was beginning to evolve. In 586 B.C.E. Israel was destroyed by Nebuchadnezzar, the King of Babylonia, who had all Jews carried away in exile. It was probably during the seventy years of exile in Babylonia that prayer without sacrifice got its big push. Seventy years later King Cyrus of Persia conquered Babylon, ruled the known world and let the Jews return to their land. Under the leadership of Ezra, the scribe, and Nehemiah, the prophet, the Jews returned to their homeland, rebuilt the Temple (called the Second Temple) and set up a new Jewishly governed state (the Second Commonwealth).

While sacrifices were restarted and people still barbecued and prayed with the *Kohanim*, the local synagogue now became an important place for daily prayer and three-times-a-week Torah study. In 350 B.C.E. Alexander the Great, a Greek, took over Persia and ruled the known world. Later, along came the Roman Empire, which defeated Greece. They ruled the known world, including Judea, the name of the country set up in the Second Commonwealth. In 70 c.e. Jerusalem was again destroyed, and the Second Temple went with it.

After the destruction a few Jewish scholars whom we call the Rabbis met in a small city called Yavneh (more or less where Ben Gurion Airport is today). They tried to figure out how to reorganize Judaism so it could survive without a Temple and without a capital. Their discussions, when spliced together with earlier discussions and those that followed, became a work known as the Talmud.

Among the things that the Rabbis decided was that *tefillah* (prayer) would have to function as the replacement for *avodah* (sacrifices). *Avodah* really means "work" or "service". They decided to consider *tefillah* as *avodat ha-lev*, (the service of the heart or heart-work).

In particular, the Rabbis decided that a chain of *brakhot* would be said three times a day as a replacement for the daily sacrifices. This chain of *brakhot* was called three different names: (1) *Ha-Tefillah*, which means "the Prayer," because it was to be the prayer that replaced sacrifice. (2) *Amidah*, the "Standing Prayer" because these *brakhot* were said silently in a standing position. (3) *Shmonah-Esrai*, the Eighteen *Brakhot*, was eighteen *brakhot* long. Later a nineteenth *brakhah* was inserted as an emergency measure, Today, even though we call it the *Shmonah-Esrai*, the chain still hads nineteen *brakhot* in it.

The Origins of the Amidah

We learn in the Talmud, *Megillah* 17b, that the *brakhot* of the *Amidah* were written by the Rabbis, specifically by Shimon the Cotton Seller, who arranged them in Yavneh during the time when Rabban Gamliel headed the Sanhedrin. In that same passage a second story is also told. It states that 125 elders, many of whom were prophets, wrote and arranged the *Amidah*.

 BREAK INTO GROUPS. THINK SILENT MOVIE. MAKE A SILENT MOVIE OF THE HISTORY OF THE AMIDAH USING PANTOMIME AND TITLE BOARDS.

 BREAK INTO GROUPS. BRAINSTORM YOUR OWN LIST OF EIGHTEEN THINGS YOU WANT TO ASK GOD FOR.

The Torah Service

The Torah service is like a visit to Mt. Sinai. We rise and reenact the Torah being given to the Jewish people. The Torah service breaks into three parts:

- Taking out the Torah.
- Reading the Torah.
- Returning the Torah.

It becomes much larger on Shabbat

Most of the Torah service is an assemblage of biblical verses. At the center of it is a passage from the Book of Numbers, Chapter 10, that describes the travel of the Ark.

They marched from Mt. Sinai for three days.
The Ark of the Eternal's Covenant traveled three days in front of them to seek out a place to camp.
The Eternal's cloud hovered over them as they moved from the camp.

When the Ark traveled Moses said:
"Get up Eternal and scatter Your Enemies
and make the ones who hate You flee from Your face."

When it rested, Moses would say:
"Eternal, please return to the many thousands of Israel."

 WHY DID THE ISRAELITES SEND THE ARK AHEAD OF THEM?

 WHY IS THE ARK OF THE COVENANT A GREAT BACKGROUND FOR THE TORAH SERVICE?'

According to legend, the Ark contained some manna, the Ten Commandments, the broken Ten Commandments, Aaron's staff that grew flowers (a miracle) and later a copy of the Torah handwritten by Moses.

 IF YOU GOT TO FILL THE ARK (LIKE A TIME CAPSULE), WHAT THINGS WOULD YOU PUT IN IT THAT CONNECTED YOU TO GOD, POINTED TOWARD THE BEST POSSIBLE FUTURE, AND PROTECTED YOU?

 THE TORAH SERVICE IS A KIND OF DANCE. RESEARCH THE MOVEMENTS AND THEN PERFORM THE TORAH SERVICE AS A DANCE.

Said Rabbi Shimon [bar Yoḥai]:
"When the congregation takes out the Scroll of the Torah to read in it, the Heavenly Gates of Mercy are opened, and God's love is heightened." (*Zohar*)

Torah Blessings

BLESSING BEFORE READING THE TORAH

בָּרְכוּ אֶת יי הַמְבֹרָךְ

בָּרוּךְ יי הַמְבֹרָךְ לְעוֹלָם וָעֶד.

בָּרוּךְ אַתָּה יי אֱלֹהֵינוּ מֶלֶךְ הָעוֹלָם

אֲשֶׁר בָּחַר בָּנוּ מִכָּל־הָעַמִּים וְנָתַן לָנוּ אֶת־תּוֹרָתוֹ.

בָּרוּךְ אַתָּה יי נוֹתֵן הַתּוֹרָה.

Praised be You, Eternal, to whom our praise is due!
Praised be You, Eternal, to whom our praise is due, to eternity and beyond!
We praise You, Eternal God, Sovereign of the universe,
Who chose us from among all people by giving us the Torah.
We praise You, Eternal, Who gives the Torah.

 HOW DO YOU FEEL ABOUT THE PHRASE "WHO CHOSE US FROM AMONG ALL PEOPLE"? MANY CONGREGATIONS REWORK ITS WORDING.

BLESSING AFTER READING THE TORAH

בָּרוּךְ אַתָּה יי אֱלֹהֵינוּ מֶלֶךְ הָעוֹלָם

אֲשֶׁר נָתַן לָנוּ תּוֹרַת אֱמֶת וְחַיֵּי עוֹלָם נָטַע בְּתוֹכֵנוּ.

בָּרוּךְ אַתָּה יי נוֹתֵן הַתּוֹרָה.

We praise You, Eternal God, Sovereign of the Universe,
Who has given us a Torah of truth,
Who has implanted within us eternal life.
We praise You, Eternal, Who gives the Torah.

 HOW DO YOU FEEL ABOUT THE PHRASE "WHO IMPLANTED WITHIN US ETERNAL LIFE"? WHAT DO YOU THINK IT MEANS?

This is an Ashkenazic Torah cover.

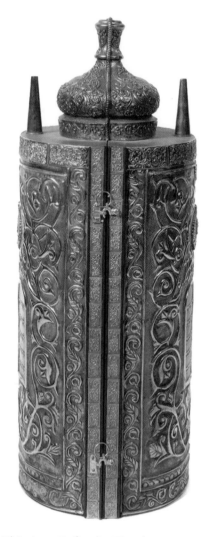

This is a Sefardic Torah cover.

 DESIGN (AND PERHAPS CONSTRUCT) A TORAH COVER OF YOUR OWN.
WORK ALONE OR IN GROUPS.

The Concluding Service

Different services end in different ways. No matter what else is present, there are two elements that are always present: the *Aleinu*, which is the final production number for the service, and the Mourner's *Kaddish*, which is a prayer about connecting to God after a death.

PRETEND YOU DON'T KNOW HOW A SERVICE ENDS. CREATE YOUR OWN ENDING THAT GOES FROM THE END OF THE TORAH SERVICE THROUGH PEOPLE LEAVING. THEN OPEN UP THE SIDDUR AND LOOK AT THE ENDING YOUR CONGREGATION USES. COMPARE YOUR ORIGINAL ENDING TO THE WAY YOUR CONGREGATION ENDS A SERVICE.

Aleinu

The *Aleinu* is like the big stage production that brings back all the high points of a big Broadway show. It is the finale of the service. It starts out thanking God for creating things (**creation**), then thanking God for having a relationship with Israel (**revelation**). We go on with thanking God for all God has done for us throughout history (**redemption**). The *Aleinu* is like a final friendship circle for the service. We all stand and echo the *Shema* with "On that day the Eternal should be one and God's name shall be one." When everything we have dreamed about (and asked for in the *Amidah*) has happened, the Jewish people's job is over. When we have peace, freedom, prosperity and all that—then the job is done.

SIDDUR SCAVENGER HUNT—OPEN UP YOUR CONGREGATIONAL SIDDUR AND FIND THE FOLLOWING. THEN FIND THE MATCHING PHRASE IN THE *ALEINU*.

Creation _____ _____

Revelation _____ _____

Redemption _____ _____

God is One _____ _____

Mourner's Kaddish

Before we go home, we remember that life doesn't go on forever. People do die. There is only so much time we have to do all we want. Friends and family may die as we grow older. We mourn and miss them, but we know that life must go on. We remember them and let them live in our memory. We praise God and know that life must go on.

We face death by praising the living God. We know that because God is within each of us, that peace will eventually come. The Kaddish never mentions death. It just praises God. In a sense it is saying that because peace will come for the world, it will come for the mourners as well.

 THERE IS A TRADITION TO WELCOME MOURNERS NEAR THE BEGINNING OF THE FRIDAY NIGHT SERVICE. IS IT BETTER TO ALLOW TIME FOR MOURNERS AT THE BEGINNING OR THE END OF SERVICES?

 WRITE A LIST OF FIVE PEOPLE YOU MISS BECAUSE THEY ARE DEAD. YOU DO NOT HAVE TO PERSONALLY KNOW THESE PEOPLE, BUT START WITH PEOPLE YOU DID KNOW. THEN SHARE YOUR LIST, EXPLAINING WHAT EACH PERSON MEANS TO YOU, WITH ANOTHER MEMBER OF YOUR CLASS.